With gratitude to
Kings Heath, Birmingham, the parish which
taught me to pray and whose prayers continue
to support and sustain me.

First published in 2018 by Alive Publishing Ltd
Graphic House, 124 City Road, Stoke on Trent, ST4 2PH
Tel: +44 (0) 1782 745600 • Fax: +44 (0) 1782 745500
www.alivepublishing.co.uk
email: booksales@alivepublishing.co.uk

© 2018 Alive Publishing. British Library Catalogue-in-
Publication Data.
A catalogue record for this book is available from the
British Library.

Imprimatur: Archbishop Bernard Longley, 2018.
Nihil Obstat: Fr Paul Dean MA, STB, MA. The nihil
obstat and imprimatur are official declarations that a
book or pamphlet is free from doctrinal or moral error.
No implication is contained therein that those who have
granted the nihil obstat or imprimatur agree with the
content, opinions or statements expressed.

ISBN: 978-1-906278-28-1

Prayers Before the Blessed Sacrament

Prayers Before the Blessed Sacrament

Timothy Menezes

alive Publishing

CONTENTS

CONTENTS

CONTENTS

PREFACE

Since I have always had an interest in the liturgy, and have studied its principles and for so much of my life as a priest have been asked to teach others about it, writing prayers has also been part of my ministry: prayers for the Blessing of new buildings; prayers for the Blessing of houses and families; prayers for Wedding Anniversaries and so on. I enjoy that creative expression which so often depends so much upon the circumstances for which the prayer is required.

Prayer before the Blessed Sacrament is, for some, a comfortable and preferred choice and, for others, a struggle and something of an endurance, at the end of which they are not sure what was achieved.

In reflecting on this form of prayer, I have come to understand that, rather like the Church's understanding of the moments around the reception of Holy Communion at Mass, deeply personal but not private, coming before the Lord in a time of adoration is praying with the

PREFACE

Church and uniting ourselves with Christ, with the family of faith and with the human family.

I was once introduced to an ecumenical initiative called 'Just Listen'. It asked people to consider the art of listening to others and not seeking to give advice of any kind. It was based upon the fact that, for most people in any kind of need, it is not even direction that they seek but the knowledge that somebody is listening to them. Loneliness in society has been likened to serious illness, and the idea that somebody could give an hour or so to say to another: I am here to listen to you, without judgement, without answers, has been seen to provide a level of response to the problems of loneliness, isolation and frustration.

Prayer before the Blessed Sacrament is a very precious form of just listening - and the listening is done by Jesus himself. The idea of God speaking to us in prayer is a difficult concept. Coming before the Lord, present for us, more capable than human beings of listening to more than one person at a time, and knowing that we can place before him the things most precious to us, not worrying about trustworthiness, is a form of prayer that can be of solace and strength to any Christian.

'I invite all Christians, everywhere, at this very moment, to a renewed personal encounter with Jesus Christ, or at least an openness to letting him encounter them; I ask all of you to do this unfailingly each day. No one should think that this invitation is not meant for him or her, since "no one is excluded from the joy brought by the Lord"' (Pope Francis, The Joy of the Gospel).

GETTING STARTED

It is likely that, to have chosen to come to prayer, you have either something to ask of God or something to be thankful for in prayer. That is the real starting-point and it is more important than how you pray.

Pray in the way that works for you

The lives of the saints or the example of people we know might be helpful to us, but they should never become a challenge for us. As God speaks to each of us in different ways, so approaches to prayer are different.

Place and Time

These have a bearing on our prayer, but for prayer before the Blessed Sacrament they might well be limited to certain hours of the day and a certain place.

Posture in Prayer

There is something about humbling ourselves in the presence of God, whether by genuflecting or kneeling. However, where those actions are not possible, then bowing and then sitting down, or varying posture between kneeling and sitting should lead us to a level of comfort so that our posture does not become a hindrance to our prayer.

Focus for Prayer

The Blessed Sacrament in the Tabernacle (a dwelling-place for God) or in the Monstrance (the holy object used to 'show' the Real Presence of Christ) is the same Eucharist that is shown to us accompanied by the words of Christ in the Mass.

For one person, the Tabernacle or the Monstrance becomes the focus; for another, eyes closed but knowing God's Presence to be before you is a way of concentrating; and for another, the reading of Scripture, or the Divine Office or another text of your choice is a way.

To come before the Lord in this prayer is to find the balance between being in awe of the immensity of God our Master and talking to a friend.

GETTING STARTED

Structure of Prayer

The norm for Prayer before the Blessed Sacrament is silent prayer.

It is always good to begin with a time of thanksgiving to God for blessings received from God or answers to prayer.

A short passage of Scripture is an obvious way to listen to the voice of the Lord. This can be the reading of today's Mass; or a book of the Bible you might be interested in. It can be one line from Scripture that either means something to you already or which you wish to centre on. Repeating it or contemplating it slowly, word by word, can be helpful.

Then you can pray for the needs of others. Our prayer is often so much more focused when we look to the needs of others before our own.

You can then look to your own needs. Let this prayer be an opening of your heart to Christ, who in his humanity can listen to you and understand

something of the human struggle and in his divinity can intercede with his Father and our Father for the needs you bring to this time of prayer

Throughout this time of prayer, you can either pray with familiar words (the Our Father; or a prayer to Jesus, e.g., Most Sacred Heart of Jesus, I place all my trust in you) or you can simply structure your prayer as a conversation with a friend, placing before the Lord all that is in your mind and heart.

Always try to conclude a time of prayer with some words of gratitude to the Lord and an expression of hope that you will meet the Lord again in prayer very soon.

Outcomes of Prayer

The first outcome of prayer is the knowledge that, whatever time we give to prayer, the Lord uses that time, regardless of whether or not we felt the time was well spent.

GETTING STARTED

The motif of a conversation with the Lord requires both speaking and listening. In the introduction I referred to the Lord listening to us in this prayer and the consolation of being listened to.

The idea of Jesus speaking to us is a much more challenging thought. Some people have a clear sense of the Lord speaking to them; others will openly admit that they are listening but they do not hear much. Perhaps with this in mind, we know that in any conversation, in any friendship, in any relationship of trust, it takes time to build up a rapport, a pattern of communication. Most of all, it takes time and a willingness to make room in life for another person. This is true for prayer. It is a lifelong endeavour, and the more we reflect on the place and time, posture, focus and structure of our prayer, only then will outcomes be in any way possible.

PRAYING WITH THE CHURCH ON SPECIAL LITURGICAL OCCASIONS AND FEAST DAYS

Lord Jesus Christ,

We come before you as a people called to watch
and wait joyfully.

We seek to know you, to understand you
as the holy men and women, the prophets and
the saints of the Old Testament sought you.

But the greater privilege is ours:
to be in this holy place.

Make us holy, make this Advent holy and grant
us the gift of patient waiting until your glory is
fulfilled, and we are awakened to eternity.

You live and reign for ever and ever.

Amen.

ADVENT II
17-24 DECEMBER

Lord Jesus,

The days of your humble birth are approaching.

Here, in stillness we come, as Zechariah waited in silence and Elizabeth bore the child of her longing; here in humility we come as Joseph, the honourable man, fulfilled your plan and as Mary pondered her great calling.

Shower upon us and upon the world infinite peace, so that we may find with you the true meaning of your birth for the salvation of the world.

You live with the Father but dwell in our midst for ever and ever.

Amen.

THE CHRISTMAS SEASON

Jesus, Saviour of the world,

Your birth at Bethlehem brings joy to our world.

We pray earnestly that the peace you came to bring may be a reality in many hearts, homes, families and nations today.

We praise you, bless you, adore you, glorify you for you have come to us this Christmas; come into our midst as light in the darkness.

May the rays of your bright promise as God's only Son, be for us warmth and comfort as children of a loving Father.

You have been born for us, Christ the Lord.

Amen.

FEAST OF THE HOLY FAMILY IN THE CHRISTMAS SEASON

Jesus, Prince of Peace,
Son of God and Son of Mary,

You have called us to spend this precious time
with you as beloved members of your family.

You have made your home with us and we ask
that you always be part of our family life.

As we find consolation and blessing in your
presence, we ask you to watch over the whole
human family.

Give courage and strength to parents and
grandparents.
Heal the wounds of family life.
Bless married couples and protect our families.

You lived under the care of Mary and Joseph,
our Saviour now and for ever.

Amen.

1.JAN

JANUARY

SUN	MON	TUE
1	2	3
		10
16	17	

AT THE BEGINNING
OF A NEW YEAR

Lord Jesus Christ,

Yesterday, today, forever, you consecrate time
and space with your abiding presence.

Here, as we stand on the threshold of a new
year, we ask that your loving presence may
overflow into every area of our lives.

Make us a new creation; Let nothing of the past
be an obstacle to our journey with you to the
Father's House.

Stay with us, Lord, on our journey and remind
us often of your gentle, guiding hand.

You are the Lord of our lives now and forever.

Amen.

FOR THE EPIPHANY

Lord Jesus Christ,

On this great Christmas Feast, your glorious
entry into our world was made known to the
world.

Today, we acknowledge that we are yours
but that you have been born for all people.

We celebrate with our Christian brothers and
sisters around the world whose tradition keeps
this day with greater celebration than Christmas
itself.

Your Epiphany reminds us that your light shines
for all and cannot be hidden.

Let us be part of that new evangelisation:
as your light radiates in our hearts and lives,
so may we speak with enthusiasm about your
birth and its message of renewal and peace for
the waiting world.

You are the Light of the World.
Amen.

THE SEASON OF LENT

Lord Jesus,

During this holy season, we accompany you with fasting, almsgiving and prayer, not so that we can focus on these things, but to make us free to come closer to you.

Thank you for these days of grace.

Through your own forty days in the wilderness and your temptation you grew in obedience to your Father, the source of your strength and wisdom.

In this encounter with you, may we gain strength in our struggles, and be drawn into the fullness of your life, that we may see and learn the right path, and walk always in your truth.

You, the Way, the Truth and the Life, now and always.

Amen.

FOR ADULTS PREPARING FOR THE SACRAMENTS OF INITIATION

Lord Jesus Christ,

We pray for those members of our community
and for adults throughout the world who are
preparing for the next stage on their journey of
faith by receiving the Sacraments of Baptism,
Confirmation and the Eucharist.

You said to the Apostle Thomas:
Blessed are those who have
not seen and yet believe.
We thank you for your action in the world
throughout history and still in our day,
most of all in the lives of
these brothers and sisters.

May the gift of the Sacraments and the
generous response of those you call speak to
them and to their families of your goodness and
beauty and truth.

As your apostles took your message of
Good News to the nations of the earth,
so infuse us with a desire to embrace your life
and to make it known for the good of others
and the sanctification of the world.

You abide in your Church
through Sacramental signs.

Amen.

HOLY WEEK

Jesus, Lord and Saviour,

This Great Week brings us to your side in the days of your Sacred Passion and Death.

In these moments, we contemplate the supreme sacrifice which was made real for your apostles in the Last Supper, on Calvary and in their witnessing to your being laid in the Tomb.

We have walked together this journey through Lent, and the Way of the Cross.

May this, your Eucharistic Presence, make us servants of one other, selfless in giving and always united with you, the Father and the Holy Spirit, God for ever and ever.

Amen.

EASTER DAY AND
THE OCTAVE OF EASTER

Risen Jesus,

We praise you, present for us as you promised.

Death has been overcome and you have opened the gates of heaven and eternal joy.

In the days following your resurrection, the disciples saw you but did not recognise you.

Here, in the Blessed Sacrament, you appear under the form of bread and wine.

As you fed the disciples on the lakeside and reminded them that you would never abandon them, so reveal to us your Divine Mercy and your constant love.

You are alive and reign in heaven and on earth,

God for ever and ever.

Amen.

EASTER SEASON

Lord Jesus,

Risen from the tomb, new hope of all those who
have died, and powerful sign of fulfilment
of the Father's will: reveal yourself anew as
the Good Shepherd who cares for the flock
entrusted to you.

As you opened the eyes of your bewildered
followers on the road to Emmaus, so bring
your word to life for us and take away any
confusion that prevents us from living in your
light.

We thank you that you still carry the scars of
your Passion.

May your wounds and your glory be shown to
us that we may embrace the newness of your
Risen life.

Amen.

ASCENSION, PENTECOST AND TRINITY SUNDAY

Lord Jesus,

At the completion of your earthly ministry, you promised your disciples the Holy Spirit, the Comforter.

We come into your sacred presence, knowing that your entire ministry was one of obedience to your Father, in the dynamic love and power of the Holy Spirit.

Bridge for us the gulf between this earthly sphere and eternity.

May we never doubt your presence in the Sacramental life of the Church, the promise of future glory for your beloved sons and daughters, heirs to your kingdom.

Amen.

LITANY CONTEMPLATING TITLES OF CHRIST

Lord Jesus,
You are the Bread of Life,
the Light of the World,
the Door of the Sheepfold,
the Good Shepherd,
the Resurrection and the Life,
the Way, the Truth and the Life,
the True Vine.

You are my Life,
without you, I have nothing.
You are my Path, my Truth,
I believe in you.

Lord Jesus,
You are the Son of God,
the Son of Mary,
the Son of David,
The Word made Flesh,
God-with-us,

the New Adam,
the Son of Man.

You are my Life,
without you, I have nothing.
You are my Path, my Truth
I believe in you.

Lord Jesus,
You are the Alpha and the Omega,
the Lord of all,
the Prince of Peace,
the Cornerstone,
the Risen Lord,
the Saviour of the World,
the Anointed One.

You are my Life,
without you, I have nothing.
You are my Path, my Truth
I believe in you.

Amen.

ON FEASTS OF OUR LADY

Lord Jesus, Son of God and Son of Mary,
we honour you on this feast day of your beloved
Mother, your most faithful disciple.

Together with you in the glory of heaven,
Queen of Heaven, she is for us
Mother of the Church.

Faithfully, she bore you in her womb,
and generously shared you with the world.
She shared with you and blessed Joseph
the home life of Nazareth.

As woman of the Eucharist,
she stood at the foot of your Cross
as you made your ultimate sacrifice.

With your Apostles she shared in
the amazement of your Resurrection.

We come to you, Lord,
through the intercession of Mary,
faithful witness.

Amen.

ON FEASTS OF THE APOSTLES

Lord Jesus,
who first spent time alone in prayer
with the Father, and then chose
apostles to share closely in your
earthly mission:
We come before you on this
Feast of the Apostles.

We pray for the Church, and especially
for our Holy Father and our Bishop,
the Shepherds you have given us.

Your apostles were privileged to witness
your ministry, but we are challenged by you
to give everything without hesitation or doubt.

We ask that we may be ready to answer your
call today and every day.

You promise eternal life to all who are faithful
to your call.

Amen.

ON THE CELEBRATION
OF SAINTS

Lord Jesus Christ,

The Saints of every place and time have known
human frailty transformed in imitation of you
into admirable witness.
In these moments, we honour those who
have shared this experience of intimacy
with you in childhood, youth or adulthood.

The humility of the saints, in their decreasing
so that you may increase, is a model for us in
the single life, in the vocations of marriage and
parenthood, in Religious life or in Holy Orders.

Through the Sacrament of your Body and Blood
in the Mass and in moments of contemplation,
give your ordinary servants the grace to do
extraordinary things.

You are glorified in your Saints.

Amen.

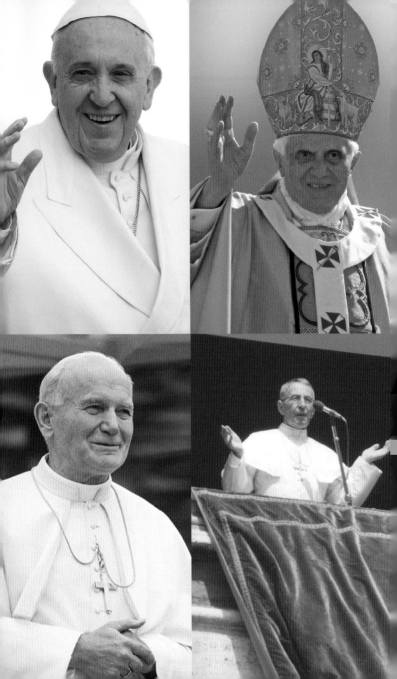

FOR THE ELECTION
OF A POPE

Lord Jesus, High Priest and Servant King,
we join with the whole Church in praying
for guidance and wisdom for those responsible
for electing a new Successor of St Peter.

We acknowledge the needs of the Church
throughout the world and the prophetic voice of
the Church in the world.

We pray for an understanding of the Church
founded on the faith of the apostles you chose,
called and sent out to every part of the world to
share your mission and your Good News.

Give to the Holy Father whom the Holy Spirit
appoints the zeal of his own ministry of deacon,
priest and bishop to lead your Church in and to
humility and holiness.

May he know that, in his weakness and his
strength, he is sustained each day as he conforms
himself to you and gives himself to his most
important task: being the Servant of the servants
of God.
Amen.

FOR THE PURIFICATION
OF THE CHURCH

Son of God and Son of Man,
you chose 12 apostles
to share your life and mission,
to live for God and to transform the world.

You chose people who were weak;
they let you down personally and they were
not always the best examples of trust in you.

We pray for your Church founded on the
witness of these frail human beings, the
apostles. Through the storms of life, we ask you
to give us courage always to do what is right.

Purify the members of your Church
of all that is evil, of all that does harm
to your name, and for the times when
we use the gift of free will wrongly.

The Church founded by you is good and true;
may those who are called to serve the Church
as ordained bishops, priests and deacons, as
consecrated religious men and women, or as
baptised lay faithful be witnesses of your truth
in the world.

For the hurt that we have caused others, may
we continue to seek forgiveness and reparation;
for the times that we have sought to protect the
Church's reputation rather than listening to its
victims we ask for a new vision of what is right.

Grant us your peace in our day and help us
always to be a voice for the voiceless.

You are the friend of the sinners and the
inspiration of Saints.

Amen.

PRAYERS FOR OTHERS

FOR PARENTS

Lord Jesus, who knew the consolation and the challenges of family life; we ask your special protection for those called to the vocation of parenthood:

You lived under the authority of your mother, Mary, and of her husband, Your Guardian, blessed Joseph, at the home in Nazareth in Galilee.

May parents always rejoice in the gift of life which you have called them to share.
May the generosity and sacrifice of parents never be taken for granted but repaid in love.
May parents always allow their children to realise their full potential without fear of jealousy or discouragement.

We ask your special blessing on those who adopt or foster children and for those who are open to the gift of being parents.

Holy Family of Nazareth. Pray for us.

Amen.

IN THANKSGIVING
FOR MARRIAGE

Loving Saviour,

We bring before your Presence today a prayer
of thanksgiving for the gift and vocation of
marriage.

We thank you for the many blessings that you
give to your people through the commitment
and dedication, the struggles and the joys of
married life.

Thank you for the witness that married people
give to the world of your love for all of your
people.

Bless and console those who are experiencing
difficulties in their marriage. Give strength to
those who support marriage through preparation
and counselling.

Keep before us always the commandments
which give life: love of God and love of
neighbour.

Amen.

FOR EXPECTANT PARENTS

Lord Jesus,

We ask your special blessing on those
who are preparing for the birth of a child.

We thank you for the gift of new life and for the
creative love with which every child changes
lives.

We know the sacredness of life at its beginning
and we ask that parents may always nurture
their children with goodness and hope.

May the dedication of parents always to do the
best for their children be a cause for thanksgiving
each day of their life.

May the safe birth of each child contribute to the
growth of the human family, and to God's family.

We ask for your blessing on all those involved
in the supervision and healthcare of the birth and
the earliest days of the lives of children.

Amen.

VOCATIONS

Lord Jesus, at the beginning of your ministry,
you called people into a relationship with you
and invited them to share in your life.

The disciples who followed you came with
their faults and failings, and these continued
even as they lived alongside you and listened to
your teaching.

You gave them insights, and those experiences
took them to the furthest reaches of the world,
and, in many cases, to give their lives in
sacrifice to you.

Here in your presence, I contemplate your
mystery in the Eucharist.

How many have taken up their Cross and
followed you and known blessings greater than
any personal achievement?

How you have blessed the parishes, schools and
families which have produced vocations to the
priesthood, to the permanent diaconate and to
consecrated life!

Touch the hearts of your people.
May parents and grandparents treasure
the gift of faith they have received.

May teachers know the value of their calling to
pass on these same treasures by the example of
their lives.

Bless the hearts and lives of religious men
and women, of deacons, priests and bishops.

Bless this generation with good and worthy
heralds of your Good News.

Amen.

Bridgettine Order

*Sisters of the
Immaculate Heart of Mary*

FOR YOUNG PEOPLE
IN THE CHURCH

Lord Jesus,
in you we find joy,
in you we find meaning for our lives.

Bless the young people whom you choose
and call to share in your life.

So many of the prophets were young,
so many of the saints found you in their
youthful search.

Your own earthly ministry bore fruit at a young
age. Give to our young people the charism of
hope and nurture the instinct of future promise.

May they learn to see that the pressures on them
will pass, but that their unique character will
endure and grow.

Fill our young people with the truth that they
can each make a real difference in life: in
their work, in their lasting friendships, in the
fulfilment of marriage, priesthood, religious life
or in serving you as individuals.

Never allow them to be discouraged by the
weary voice of despondency, but let their lives
transform others into people of hope who
always see potential.

Most of all, Lord Jesus,
keep our young people close to your heart,
and teach them always the love which
accompanies them in this life and
secures their future in heaven.

Amen.

FOR THOSE PREPARING
FOR EXAMS OR INTERVIEWS

Lord Jesus,
humble of heart,
we pray to you for those who are taking exams
or attending interviews at this time.

Give to them the peace of mind and the
eloquence to express what they know rather
than to worry about what they don't.

These events in their lives can be so important
for the direction of their lives in the future.
You prayed that the Father's will may be done
in your life. May they accept the Father's will.

We pray for those given the role of examiners
and interviewers, and we ask you to give them
discerning and generous minds.

In your ministry, you said that your followers
should not worry about what to say because
they would be given the words to speak.

Most of all, give to all those preparing for
exams and interviews a knowledge of their true
worth and the broader picture for their lives.

Do not allow the pressures on them to be
overwhelming or let them lose sight of the
perspective that success and development come
at different times for different people.

Amen.

FOR CATHOLIC TEACHERS

Lord Jesus, who taught by an example of compassion, of service, of sacrifice:

We pray for those whom you have called to shape young lives, to build the foundations for a new generation.

Give to Catholic teachers a strong sense of your purpose in their vocation.

Endow them with zeal which is renewed daily, with a reassurance of your love for them so they may always show a genuine care for the young lives entrusted to them.

May the grace given to them in prayer and in the sacraments nourish their lives and be the greatest source of wisdom and strength.

May the parables with which you taught be always fresh as they reach today's young people, tomorrow's parents, that the faith may be a treasure that is received with gratitude and passed on with conviction.

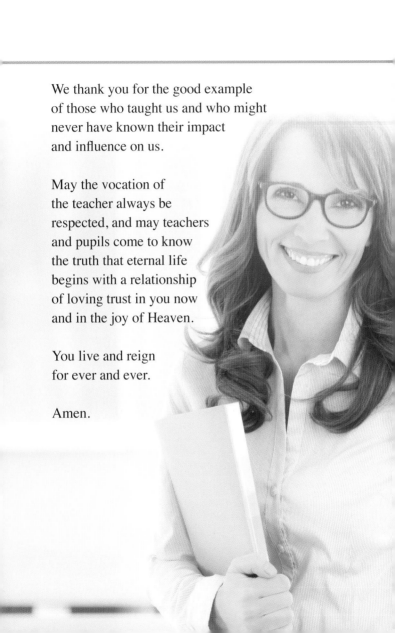

We thank you for the good example
of those who taught us and who might
never have known their impact
and influence on us.

May the vocation of
the teacher always be
respected, and may teachers
and pupils come to know
the truth that eternal life
begins with a relationship
of loving trust in you now
and in the joy of Heaven.

You live and reign
for ever and ever.

Amen.

AT THE TIME OF AN ELECTION FOR LOCAL OR NATIONAL GOVERNMENT

Lord Jesus,
whose authority on earth was often questioned,
whose power was often doubted:

We pray at this time of discernment and choice
for those seeking election in the near future.

May they recognise the qualities of integrity
and honesty as being more necessary than
desirable.

May all those who are given the privilege of
voting know their responsibility to do so.

May those on the margins of our society and
our neighbourhoods, the voiceless, find a voice
in our elected representatives.

Above all, may the knowledge of a power
greater than ourselves and an authority beyond
the confines of this life be respected for people
of faith and for the common good.

You live and reign in Heaven and on earth.
Amen.

FOR PEACE IN THE WORLD

Lord Jesus,

As you prepared for your Passion and Death, you gave to your apostles the gift of peace, a peace the world cannot give.

After your Resurrection, you appeared to the apostles and offered them anew the gift of peace.

You told your followers not to be troubled or afraid.

We pray for peace in the world.

May those who have become used to conflict taste freedom from hatred and the happiness of life and love.

May those who live in areas affected by war come to see the brightness of a hope beyond hostility.

We give thanks for your intervention in places that have left war behind and who now enjoy the promise of peace. Touch hearts, demonstrate love, offer hope.

You love the human race created by the Author of all that is good.

Amen.

FOR THOSE WHO ARE SICK

Lord Jesus,

Healer of bodies and souls,
we intercede for those who
are living with sickness.

Your own wounds of suffering during
your Passion and your agony in the garden
bring you close to all those who suffer.

Be a source of comfort and hope
to all those who carry the burden
of sickness in body or mind.

Bless all those whose vocation is to care,
whether professionally or
through the bonds of family.

May your loving gaze bring wholeness
to brokenness and light out of darkness.

Amen.

FOR THOSE LIVING WITH DEMENTIA

Lord Jesus,

You call into your company those who labour
and are overburdened.

We pray for those members of our community
who live with dementia.

We hold before you the challenges that life
presents for our brothers and sisters, for their
families and for all who offer care and respite.

May the richness of life and the gift of memory
create opportunities for joyful reflections on the
whole span of each person's life.

May the dignity of advanced age be respected,
and may the words and gestures of prayer
which have accompanied life be a reminder
of an enduring relationship with you,
their Lord and their God.

Amen.

FOR THOSE
APPROACHING DEATH

Lord Jesus,
Crucified and Risen Saviour,

We come before you as your faithful people,
praying at this time for those we know and love
who approach the end of this early life.

Through your ministry of restoring others to life
and in your own Resurrection, we know your
power to lead us beyond the deep sadness of
separation in this world to the overwhelming
joy that you promise us beyond the threshold of
death.

We believe that our bodies are Temples of your
Spirit, the recognition of uniqueness which is
given to each of God's beloved children.

Although the life to come is as yet outside our
experience, it is something familiar to you and
for which you have prepared us.

Remind those who are drawing towards the end
of their life on earth of your presence with them

on this last journey as you have accompanied
them throughout their life.

In creation, the Father saw all that he had made
and declared it to be good. Reflect your goodness
in us until our last breath.

May our leaving this world not be seen by
anybody as the end but an invitation to a life
beyond our imagining.

As you said to the man who died on the Cross
alongside you: Today you will be with me in
Paradise, so give to those whose journey beyond
this life is imminent a knowledge that you are
with them here and will be with them after death.

Let us be a people of thanksgiving for life's
blessings. As this life reaches completion
and fulfilment, the lives of others are just
beginning, as the cycles of life always lead from
death to resurrection.

You lead us to the Father and Source of all Life,
Amen.

FOR THOSE WHO
HAVE EXPERIENCED
BROKEN RELATIONSHIPS

Compassionate Lord Jesus,
you spoke to your followers of the bandaging
of the wounds of the Good Samaritan,

We call for your healing for those who are
experiencing the pain and heartache of the
breakdown of their relationship.

As they look so differently now at the love which
was shared but which has now failed to sustain
their life, we pray that they may retain a sense of
their dignity which nobody can take away.

In every breakdown of a relationship, we
recognise the circles of family affected, many
beyond their control, but who also experience the
separation from others they have known.

The separation of those who have formed bonds
of family brings lasting sorrow and regret.
It can destroy the ability to trust in others.

We ask that Mary, Our Lady of Sorrows, who
knew the challenges of motherhood and of
family life, may be especially close to those
who struggle as a result of the breakdown of a
relationship.

May they know the power of forgiveness, the
possibility of renewed hope and the desire for
them to make of each day a step towards healing
of past hurts.

You, Lord, knew pain and suffering,
disappointment, and rejection by those closest to
you, but always the loyalty of a loving Father.

Amen.

FOR THOSE WHO HAVE EXPERIENCED MISCARRIAGE OR STILLBIRTH

Lord Jesus,
you are the Son of God, yet you are close to us
in all that makes us human.

We come before you in prayer and ask for
your gift of consolation for parents who have
cherished the gift of life at its beginning.

As they come to terms with a loss that will be
part of the story of their life that shapes them,
so be close to them as you did throughout your
ministry for those who needed your healing
touch.

Bless them as mothers and fathers with the
knowledge that the child for which they hoped
is safe in your care, in the joy of your presence
and among the saints and angels who praise you
in eternity.

You are the Good Shepherd who knows each
one by name.

Amen.

FOR HOMELESS PEOPLE

Lord Jesus,

We pray for those men and women who are homeless today.

So that we might not lose sight of this being about real people, we pray for the homeless people that we have seen in the past week.

Homeless people have a face, a name, a story and, hopefully, a future.

Homeless people are somebody's sons and daughters; they are sometimes parents too.

Give to all of our brothers and sisters of the human family the dignity of a place to call home.

May we never ignore those who are in need, even if we cannot help them, because you call us to see your face in their faces, created in God's image and likeness.

Amen.

FOR PRISONERS
AND THEIR FAMILIES

Lord Jesus Christ,

You called sinners to a new way of life, to embrace forgiveness and to make reparation.

We pray for those who, on account of their faults, have been deprived of their liberty.

You taught that those who inherit the Kingdom are the ones who recognise you in those they visit in prison.

We ask that we may leave judgement to the Father of mercies; that we may be part of a society that believes always in the hope of redemption.

Be close to those who have been victims of crime.

Bless the families of those in prison and in the troubled circumstances that might not be of their making.

May all of us who bear the trace of human
sinfulness see in every child of God the
potential of a fellow citizen of heaven.

You live and reign for ever and ever.

Amen.

FOR ASYLUM SEEKERS
AND REFUGEES

Lord Jesus,
I come to you,
here in the safety of
your Father's House of Prayer,
a place where I know that I belong,
a place of safe refuge,
under your protection.

I hold before you
my brothers and sisters,
whether or not I know them by name,
who are far from their home,
displaced especially by war or conflict,
those who have nowhere to call home.

You truly know their plight:
from your birth in poverty at Bethlehem,
to your exile in Egypt for fear of Herod;

to your Crucifixion outside the city walls,
and your burial in a borrowed tomb.
Give to those who seek asylum or refuge
a knowledge of their God-given dignity.

Inspire with generosity individuals and
communities who can help to bring about a new
life and a sense of welcome.

Make our common language one of respect
and love, that when our exile here on earth
is complete, we may be in no doubt of
the homeland which is our destination:
the Kingdom prepared for us since the
foundation of the world, where you live
for ever and ever.

Amen.

IN TIME OF
NATURAL DISASTER

Lord Jesus,
you are close to the Father's heart,

We ask your prayers for all those affected by
the recent disaster.

At times like this, we struggle to understand
your place in our world, your power to save.

We implore your help for all those who have
been injured, displaced or bereaved by this
event.

We ask you to give eternal rest to those who
have lost their lives unexpectedly.

We pray especially for those whose professionalism and care will be called upon to give comfort, shelter or medical help.

When people have been left with nothing, help us to reflect on the precious gift of life itself; that we may never take it for granted and may know the privilege of receiving this gift each day.

May those in any need be given relief, and may we all honour our responsibility for the Care of Creation and for our stewardship of it.

Amen.

AFTER A TERRORIST ATTACK

Lord Jesus Christ,
meek and humble of heart, we come before you,
and we struggle to make sense of recent events.

We know that we live with
the gift of free will, but now we see the
devastation of free will put to the wrong use.

Take to yourself those who have died.
Bring healing and peace to the injured.
Give consolation to the bereaved and to
families whose lives have changed forever.

In these moments of silence and stillness,
we ask that you, who are the Prince of Peace,
may bring to our world a renewed spirit of peace.

Turn the hearts of those who live with hatred to
love.

Give to each one of us reasons to seek peace
and share your peace in our own lives, so that
peace may grow, and love may overcome fear.

Amen.

FOR VICTIMS OF ABUSE

Lord Jesus,

We recognise in these moments of prayer
the burden that people carry as a result of abuse
in their lives.

We acknowledge the many forms of abuse
and their often hidden way of affecting lives.

We pray to you for the most vulnerable
members of our society, and we pray that in
their homes and schools, hospitals and other
institutions they may experience the care they
need and the equality they deserve.

We ask for purification and forgiveness for the
Church's members who have sinned in their
duty of care towards children and young people.

Help us all to live in such a way that we never
abuse the power that is given to us.

May those who speak up for the vulnerable
always be heard, and may the weakest of voices
always know that they will be listened to.

Heal your people.
Heal the victims of abuse.
Heal your Church.

Amen.

FOR THOSE WHO CANNOT PRAY

Lord Jesus,
here in our midst, present among your people,
we pray for those who find prayer difficult or
impossible, for any reason:

For those who are living with sickness
and who cannot concentrate on prayer;
for those who are struggling with faith
and are not inclined to prayer;
for those who try hard to pray
but find it an empty experience.

It is our privilege today to offer our humble
prayer for those who cannot pray, just as at
times we depend on the prayers of others for us.
Be close to your people wherever they are
and in whatever circumstances you find them.

As your love and power cannot be contained
by space and time, extend your protection
to the whole human family, as it seeks to serve
the common good.

You live and reign for ever and ever.
Amen.

FOR THE FAITHFUL DEPARTED

Lord Jesus,

Our resurrection and our life,
we entrust to your safekeeping
those we know and love who have died.

As we contemplate the mystery of
the Incarnation, through which
you shared our human life,
and the mystery of the Cross and Resurrection,
we ask you to give eternal rest to those
who have completed their earthly journey.

We pray for those who have
nobody to pray for them,
and we look forward to
the day of Resurrection.

You are the fountain of life and love.

Amen.

PERSONAL PRAYERS

IN NEED OF PEACE

Lord Jesus Christ,

I have chosen to spend this time in your company, in your Presence.

Give me the gift of peace.

In these moments, invite me to enter more deeply into your love, your consolation.

My life can be so busy, so active, so demanding. People can demand so much of me.

In this silence and stillness, let your heart speak to my heart.

I ask nothing more than the gift of your peace to strengthen me for all that is in my heart today.

Lord Jesus, I trust in you.

Amen.

IN THANKSGIVING

Lord Jesus,
when only one of the ten cured of a serious
illness returned to give thanks for the cure,
you asked: the others, where are they?

In these moments of stillness in your presence,
I know that I have so much for which to be
thankful. So often, I come before you to ask for
favours. Today, I recognise the blessings of my
life, these days of grace, when your life has been
made known to me.

I thank you for your generous gift of yourself
to me and to all people, made present here and in
the tabernacles of the world.

Make of me a person of gratitude for your
goodness. May my life become for others a
witness to your love for your people, so that all
may come to see the promises you offer every
day in every place.

You who embody thanksgiving in your Risen
life.
Amen.

FOR MY FAMILY

Lord Jesus,

From your birth at Bethlehem,
you came to know home and family life in
Nazareth.

You grew in wisdom and knowledge,
you experienced human care,
you knew disappointment and frustration.

I entrust my family to your care today:
their joys and sorrows,
their challenges and their successes.

My family know me well,
and sometimes they know me too well.

St Augustine of Hippo spoke of God
being closer to me than I am to myself.

Bless each member of my family,
and give me the reassurance that
the bonds of family are a gift.

Bring your healing to any
conflict within my family.

May forgiveness be the
medicine that guides us
through the difficulties that arise.

May the family I have been given,
the heritage that has shaped me,
and the prayers of your
Holy Family accompany me
and all those I carry in my heart.

Amen.

BEFORE THE SACRAMENT
OF RECONCILIATION

O my God,
because you are so good,
I am sorry that I have sinned against you;
and by the help of your grace I will not sin again.

With these words, Lord Jesus, I prepare for
an encounter with your merciful love in the
Sacrament of Reconciliation.

I ask for the grace to reflect with honesty on my
life and to make a good confession.

I ask for the courage not to be afraid as I seek
your compassion for my failure to show love to
you, my God, to my family and friends, to those
with whom I live and work and to myself.

I ask your blessing on the priest who will be the
channel of your mercy for me in this Sacrament.

May I come to know your pardon and peace
and the new life that you offer me as you did for
the paralytic in the Gospel. You are the Lord of
life and of mercy.
Amen.

IN THE AUTUMN OF LIFE

Lord Jesus,
the same: yesterday, today and for ever;

I ask for the wisdom which has
always accompanied me but which
I need to know more than ever now.

In your relatively short earthly life,
you spoke to people of all ages, you gave
to each the dignity of their state of life.

Help me to celebrate my life so far
and give thanks for the many blessings that you
make known to me and, to others, through me.

I ask for the acceptance of any limitations that
now form part of the person you call me to be.

Where physical weakness frustrates me,
let me know my value in your sight and in the
lives of others;
where my ability to remember is
not as strong as it was, reassure me of
my worth to live in the present moment.

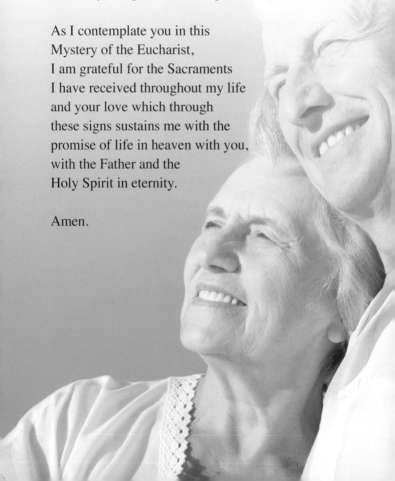

As the world around me seems at times so
different from the experiences of my youth and
adult life, may I see the changes around me as
creativity and growth and inspiration.

As I contemplate you in this
Mystery of the Eucharist,
I am grateful for the Sacraments
I have received throughout my life
and your love which through
these signs sustains me with the
promise of life in heaven with you,
with the Father and the
Holy Spirit in eternity.

Amen.

IN TIME OF FEAR OR DOUBT

Lord of my Life,
I come into your presence aware of my human
weakness, conscious of my fear and doubt.

I am fearful of the future and I do not feel in
control of what will happen. I doubt myself and
my ability to cope.

Here I am, in your presence, who surrendered all
power and control; who expressed fear of what
was to come and asked that, if possible, the cup
of suffering might pass you by.

I come into your presence with the honesty of
my doubt and fear.

I ask simply that you console me with your
healing presence. Give me the grace to accept
your will and to know that, with you at my side
on this journey, I need not be afraid of what is to
come.

Overshadow my doubt with hope.
Overcome my fear with love.
Amen.

IN TIME OF DISAPPOINTMENT

Lord Jesus,
brother and friend,

How often you experienced disappointment
in your mission to make
the Father's will known on earth;
the frequent disappointment brought
about by the frailty of the apostles;
the constant disappointment that religious
leaders either could not or would not understand
you; the ultimate disappointment that the world
preferred darkness to your light.

In this time of disappointment for me
or for those closest to me,
help me to remember the words
'thy will be done'.

At the moment, things have not
gone to plan for me.

Help me to move beyond regret
and to reach for the next opportunity.

Allow me to see that disappointment
can pass and that soon I may come
to know your purpose for me.

At this time, give me the grace
not to dwell on past hurts
but to trust in your promises.

If it is possible,
give me the humility
to be glad for the
successes of others.

Amen.

IN TIME OF
PERSONAL DIFFICULTY

Lord of hope,
companion on the journey of life,
You said: Come to me,
all who are burdened,
and I will give you rest.

I come to spend time with you,
to rest in your presence,
and to renew my sense of purpose.
In these moments of struggle,
help me to remember the blessings of my life:
people, experiences, hopes - all of which
can easily fade from my mind when difficulties
come my way.

When the problems of life overwhelm me,
remind me that I am a child of God
who is never alone.

When the way ahead is not clear,
or I fear that I cannot achieve the things that
others expect of me, teach me to take time to
reflect on past achievements, on the goodness
that others have shown to me.

Jesus, my Saviour and my friend, today is a gift.
Help me to use today and to know that I can
only do my best to face the challenges of
this day.

I trust in your goodness.
Lead me and guide me.

Amen.

FOR A PERSON WHO CANNOT RECEIVE HOLY COMMUNION

Lord Jesus,
I come before you and ask for an outpouring of
love in your presence.

You gave yourself at the Last Supper and on the
Cross of Calvary for your apostles and for the
many.

Your sacrifice is made present on the altar
at every Mass and its fruits remain here
for prayer in precious moments like this.

As I place my life before you,
I ask to draw strength from you for my family
and all those I love as well as for myself.
May I never doubt my worthiness in your sight
as I seek to live the life of faith as fully as I can.

Continue to make known your will for me
and help me to know that at every Mass I attend
and whenever I come before you in Adoration,
I am blessed with the graces of your Passion,
Death and Resurrection simply by being here.

Amen.

FOR A PERSONAL COMMITMENT TO EVANGELISATION

Light of the Nations,
Teacher of Truth,

You called your followers to go out to the
whole world and proclaim the Good News.

Although my faith is something personal,
I know that I am called to share this gift.

Let the focus of evangelisation not be what I
have to say, but let me be aware of the power of
my words and actions to reflect my faith in you.

May I recognise the many areas of society
who do not know your life, your mission here
on earth or your place in Heaven as promises
for every person.

When I do not feel confident in my faith,
may I rise to the challenge of going beyond fear

and doubt to see that my simple words of trust
in you and the knowledge of your love for me
might be the difference today between despair
and hope for another person:
a friend, a colleague, a member of my own
family who might hear these words as an
invitation, a lifeline.

May each day given to me to do your will
be an opportunity for me to recognise the
consolation of faith which others can receive
through me and through all those you call to
serve you.

You are the Word, in the beginning with the
Father, who have spoken to many hardened
hearts and opened the eyes of faith, and who
promised that the Spirit would remain always
with the Church.

Amen.

IN TIME OF BEREAVEMENT

Lord Jesus Christ,
I come before you at a time of sorrow and loss.

You are the fulness of life, because through
your death and rising to life, you lead us to
eternal joy in the Father's Kingdom.

Be close to me and to my family,
and give us the knowledge that
our brother/sister is safe in your care.

The end of life is a moment of departure
from so much of what we know and love.

Help me to enter into these moments where you
are close to me. You are also in the Father's
presence, with all those who have lived this life
and are now with God.

Your presence in the Eucharist
is my strength for the journey through life.
Your nourishment here is also
a promise that all that follows this life
is peace and joy for ever.

May I treasure the memories of loved ones here
and look forward to my reunion with them
beyond suffering, beyond sadness at the
banquet with all the saints who have known you
in this life and now share in the fulness of your
presence.

Eternal rest grant unto (name), O Lord,
and let perpetual light
shine upon him/her.
May he/she rest in peace.

Amen.

SUICIDE OF A FAMILY
MEMBER OR FRIEND

Loving and compassionate Jesus,
I come before you with the deepest sadness
and with so many questions.

In my confusion, I have also known anger
and guilt: things I could have done
to avoid this, anger at my loss.

I need to know that the person I care about
is safe from harm and in your care.

Here, in moments of silence and stillness,
I stand before the Mystery of your Presence,
which requires the eyes of faith
to understand what the world cannot see.

I stand too before the mystery of death,
which feels like it has robbed me
of something so dear to me.

Help me to accept that there are questions today
to which I might never know answers
in this life, wounds that will never heal
completely. Be close to me and my family.

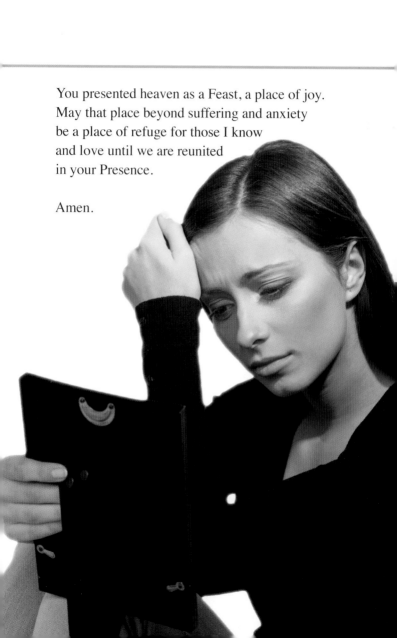

You presented heaven as a Feast, a place of joy.
May that place beyond suffering and anxiety
be a place of refuge for those I know
and love until we are reunited
in your Presence.

Amen.

PRAYER INTENTIONS

PRAYER INTENTIONS

IMAGE CREDITS

IMAGE CREDITS